Hindu Gods

Hindu Gods
The Spirit of the Divine

by Priya Hemenway

CHRONICLE BOOKS

SAN FRANCISCO

Library of Congress Cataloging-in-Publication Data:
Hemenway, Priya.
Hindu gods : the spirit of the divine / By Priya Hemenway.
p. cm.
ISBN 0-8118-3645-2
1. Gods, Hindu. 2. Hinduism. 3. Hinduism—Sacred books. I. Title.
BL1210 .H38 2003
294.5'211—dc21
2002005176

Manufactured in China

Designed by Jim Benson

Distributed in Canada by Raincoast Books
9050 Shaughnessy Street
Vancouver, British Columbia V6P 6E5

10 9 8 7 6 5 4 3 2 1

Chronicle Books LLC
85 Second Street
San Francisco, California 94105

www.chroniclebooks.com

Page 2: Expressing the spirit of all that is divine, the Hindu gods are love incarnate.
In era after era, Vishnu fondly caresses his beloved.

This book is dedicated to all those who walk along the path of truth, wherever it goes.

CONTENTS

Shiva and Parvati have descended from their home on Mount Kailash and are entertained by a group of dancers and musicians. For Hindus, gods and humans are part of one existence, serving each other in the search for truth and liberation.

Introduction

Whenever a devotee wishes, with unwavering faith, to worship me in a particular form, I take that form.
    —Bhagavad Gita 4.1

HINDUISM IS THE NAME GIVEN TO THE SPIRITUAL BELIEFS that have inspired the people of India for thousands of years. While often thought of as a religion, Hinduism differs profoundly from other religions in that there is no single founder, no savior, no dogma of belief, and no prescribed ritual or rule of practice. Hinduism is known to its people as Santana Dharma, the eternal religion, for it remains eternally alive in the hearts of those who seek to know themselves.

The spirit of the Hindu gods is as eternal as the desire to seek truth. The gods are gifts from what Hindus call nirvana—the state of absolute freedom, God, liberation, or truth. Kept alive in the hearts of Hindus through centuries of storytelling, these gods breathe humanity and humor into an everyday religiousness. They breathe understanding into existential questions and wisdom into all aspects of life.

Hinduism has its roots in one of the world's first known civilizations, which began more than five thousand years ago in northern India and Pakistan. Over time this civilization expanded to include the whole of the Indian subcontinent. In their early days, the Hindus were an agrarian people living along the banks of the Indus and the Sarasvati Rivers, separated from the rest of the world by the huge Himalayas. The early civilization was a thriving one—until a dramatic shift in weather, sometime in the second millennium B.C.E., caused the Sarasvati River to dry up, forcing the people who lived along its banks to migrate in great numbers.

This migration, along with the desire to extend the boundaries of known worlds, led the early Hindus to interact with other emerging civilizations. Their thoughts and concepts spread, mixing and merging with those of other peoples, continuing always to change. The outstanding quality of Hinduism, and that which has contributed most to its survival, is the ability of its followers to embrace and learn from everything.

Much of what we know about these early people has been gleaned by archaeologists digging at the sites of their early cities and corroborated by the Vedas and the Upanishads, ancient verses that serve as the backbone for the Hindu religion.

Passed on by word of mouth over centuries, the stories and legends of Hinduism have become long epics filled with great insight. Thousands of years of singing and chanting, weaving together tales of reality with tales of fantasy, informing both with an evolving spirituality, and illustrating everything with a highly expressive art—all this has contributed to that which we call Hinduism.

Throughout India small temples are built into the landscape. It is a country where everything is considered to be holy and it is the longing of every heart to reach nirvana.

TRANSFORMATION OF THE SOUL
THE BELIEFS OF HINDUISM

From the unreal, lead me to the real!
From the darkness, lead me to the light!
From death, lead me to immortality!
—Brhadaranyaka Upanishad 1.3.28

LIKE ALL RELIGIONS, HINDUISM IS BASED ON inquiries into the nature and purpose of human existence. Hindu belief is centered on the transformation of the soul, a process connected to an evolution that happens over many lifetimes.

Nirvana is the ultimate illumination. It frees one from all suffering, from death and rebirth, and from all other worldly bonds, and is the experience of the seer. The seer is one who through many lives has become purified, having cleansed the heart, the mind, and the body of distraction. The seer sees clearly and has a direct experience of the eternal soul—that which is so subtly hidden in the world, that which is so obvious but nearly impossible to glimpse.

Believing that life is a constant process of lessons to learn, Hindus seek understanding that will give them the eyes and heart to see clearly. They search for experiences that will lead them from the unreal to the real, from the temporal to the eternal, from that which appears to be false toward that which is ultimately true. The practices of Hinduism revolve around creating possibilities through which a person slowly, slowly awakens.

There are several different paths, or practices, that Hindus observe to reach this state. Centering their attention on God, or some aspect of God, in an affair of the deepest love and devotion, ultimately they experience their own divinity.

Losing the self in the love of God is not something that happens easily, but rather is the work of many lives. Hindus have developed a deep understanding of the laws of transmigration and devote themselves to their transformation. From the formal rituals that take place in temples to the spontaneous utterings of prayer, Hindus are dedicated to the love of God.

UNLOCKING THE DOOR TO THE DIVINE
WORSHIP

To HINDUS, THE CONCEPT OF WORSHIP is beautiful. It is the way in which a human being participates in the unfolding of the universe. For a person dedicated to transformation, worship is an integral part of life. Over thousands of years worship has become a complex phenomenon consisting of highly evolved rituals and esoteric practices.

Techniques of meditation and yoga are being taught in the West now, and through them we can sample the extent to which worship stills the mind and prepares one to move inward. Other methods include chanting mantras (sacred formulas that tap deeply into the nature of sound), visualizing yantras (esoteric drawings that serve as symbolic keys to concepts that cannot be adequately expressed in words), and performing mudras (highly developed movements that encourage awareness of the senses). For Hindus, these techniques are all completely interwoven into the fabric of daily life.

Hindus treat every aspect of life as divine, and their days are full of observances and rituals where music and chanting accompany symbolic offerings. Beginning by greeting God in the rising sun and ending with lighting lamps with sacred fire as night falls, Hindus continually meet the many forms of God.

Festivals are given over to the gods, shrines are dedicated to them, songs are sung and music composed for them, while dances and dramas enact the themes of their lives. Stores and streets are named after them. Food and drink are received with thanks to them. Seemingly endlessly, the gods are remembered and celebrated.

Homes and public places are full of small altars to various gods. Kitchens are host to the divinity that nourishes through food, sleeping rooms to that which pervades in sleep. With all of this, it is not surprising that when Hindus build formal stonework temples, they are compelling. To the initiated, the Hindu temple holds powerful keys to unlocking the door of the divine, for it is the temple of the heart that finally dissolves into God. Every aspect of temple architecture perfects and supports this experience.

TALES OF THE GODS
THE RELIGIOUS TEXTS OF HINDUISM

THE WORD "HINDUISM" REFERS TO A WAY OF LIFE. It draws its wisdom neither from a single prophet or sage nor from a single holy book, but from thousands of years of collective wisdom—wisdom that continues to be passed on in the ever popular tradition of storytelling. Many villages in India have their storytellers, and in the evenings people gather together to listen to the tales of the gods. The scriptures have their place in the temples and the ashrams of gurus (teachers), and Hindus have great respect for this aspect of belief. But what contributes most to keeping the beliefs of Hindusim alive is the repeated recounting of the escapades and tales of their gods.

Puja is the name for a religious ceremony in which food, flowers, incense, and water establish the connection with God. Here a tree is worshipped by a group of women who perceive God to be present everywhere.

The earliest Hindu scriptures to be written down were the sacred texts of the Vedas. No one knows when they were composed, but they were passed on orally from generation to generation for thousands of years, eventually being written down around 1500 B.C.E. The Vedas are a collection of hymns and chants sung by priests to gods that are barely recognizable now, for time has given them different faces and different names. The scriptures include complex formulas for rituals, along with an enormous body of sacred teachings.

Shortly after the Vedas were written, the Upanishads were composed. More philosophical in nature, the Upanishads delve deeply into the nature of the soul. They reveal the spiritual insights of the first gurus. The word *upanishad* means "at the feet of," for the scriptures were first spoken to disciples sitting at the feet of these early teachers.

The great epics were written sometime later—between 400 B.C.E. and 600 C.E. The Ramayana and the Mahabharata are based on stories surrounding the constant, mythical inner battle between the soul and the senses.

The Ramayana tells the tale of Rama, an incarnation of Vishnu, and his triumph over the demon-king Ravana. In twenty-four thousand verses the complex struggle between good and evil is described, weaving itself around a fascinating study of karma—the consequence of past deeds. The tale concludes with a sublime statement on the purpose of life.

The Mahabharata is four times longer than the Ramayana. Its main theme is again the struggle between good and evil, this time exemplified by two families. The famous passage within the Mahabharata called the Bhagavad Gita contains instructions from the god Krishna (an incarnation of Vishnu) to the warrior Arjuna on the eve of a battle he is destined to fight. In its scope and profundity, the complete Mahabharata is comparable to the Bible or the epics of Homer.

Tales of Krishna's early life are told in the
Bhagavata Purana. Here, with his brother,
Balarama, and a group of cowherds he ap-
proaches a palm grove that is guarded by
Dhenuka, a cannibal demon who is reputed to
eat anyone who approaches.

The last of the major religious texts to appear were the Puranas, the great storehouse of Hindu mythology. The word *purana* means "ancient narrative," and the Puranas are the tales of the gods. From these tales the great Hindu triad of Brahma, Shiva, and Vishnu emerges.

SERVING MANKIND
THE GODS AND THEIR TEACHINGS

By some counts there are 330 million gods in the Hindu pantheon. This great palette is, like life, vividly colored and infinitely varied. It is often difficult to distinguish one god from another. Contemplating the nature of the divine, Hindus see every aspect of life included. Through the image of each god, God is worshiped. Through the worship of their gods, Hindus move closer to the divine. This is the gift of the gods. They are such an integral part of daily life that life itself becomes holy.

The most significant stories of the gods revolve around the eternal dynamic of creation and destruction, the basic process of life. Brahma is the creator and Shiva is the destroyer. Together with Vishnu, the preserver, these three gods form the basic trinity of Hinduism. Married to them, in different manifestations, is the feminine spirit of *shakti*—the energy that gives rise to all existence.

Brahma, Shiva, and Vishnu appear over and over in these stories, taking on different personae at different times, for like nature they are not

Shiva rides upon his mount, the white bull Nandi, the Lord of Joy and a symbol of fertility. The many aspects of Shiva include the young ascetic, the cosmic dancer, the lord of destruction, and the benevolent protector and loving husband. In his hands Shiva holds a trident and a spear. Their long handles represent the two axes of the universe.

fixed. The three gods and their female counterparts have human emotions and complex relationships. Sometimes angry, sometimes calm, they are supreme. Hundreds and thousands of other gods support and color the great triad, reflecting life in its many aspects—from trees and animals to emotions and desires. The gods live on sacred mountains together and visit earth in times of need or distress.

Each god is replete with a complex set of symbols and tales. In paintings and sculptures the gods are shown with multiple faces and multiple arms, their hands carrying tools specific to them. They ride symbolic mounts that represent their powers and are clothed and colored in ways that suggest their qualities.

With compassion and patience the gods serve mankind, sometimes torn with grief by the difficulty of this task. The spirit of the Hindu gods is an understanding spirit. It is a spirit that guides humans to nirvana or the experience of God.

While serving foremost to transform the lives of those who worship them, the gods of Hinduism also serve simply to instruct and inspire. Their complex relationships and their numerous exploits are the subject of stories that are told over and over to the young, so that a Hindu child grows up learning many of the subtle inferences that lie within the tales.

The following pages tell the stories of Brahma, Vishnu, and Shiva and introduce, as well, a few of the most important gods and goddesses of Hinduism. May this book provide you with a lasting flavor of what this extraordinary and ancient religion offers to the adept and the hopeful. May it inspire in you a greater understanding of and ever more tolerant attitude toward our very human nature.

Krishna is pictured here with his beloved Radha, a cowgirl. Their love and devotion to one another has become an allegory for the great love that exists between the gods and those who worship them.

Shiva performs the cosmic Dance of Bliss while Brahma (left) and Vishnu (right) provide musical accompaniment. The movement of the universe is maintained through the regular rhythm of this dance, called Nataraja, while gods, demons, and all supernatural creatures look on in wonder. Occasionally there is a pause in the music while Shiva looks for a new rhythm. At that moment the universe ends, to be re-created as the music begins again.

The Eternal Triad

ACCORDING TO HINDU SCRIPTURES, THE POSSIBILITY OF LIFE as we know it depends upon a place and a time in which it can exist. The universe we live in is but one small aspect of reality, but it is the one that most concerns us.

Having probed deeply into the nature of things, the early Hindu seers described creation as having emerged from a divine essence, which they called Brahman. This divine essence is formless; it is the void that Hindus call God. Descending into the realms of existence, Brahman is perceived as three energies that create and maintain life—Brahma, Vishnu, and Shiva. By giving names to these energies, the early seers of Hinduism began the creation of their many myths—myths that act as a bridge between that which we perceive and that which we cannot know. The gods are not God; they simply represent the energies that make up life.

The Hindu gods are born of an impulse to know. Thus, the firstborn, Brahma, is the source of all knowledge. He is the seed, the creator of the universe. He is not actively worshiped, because his work is done. However, Vishnu, who is the preserver of things, is often worshiped by those who have an interest in the pleasures of life. He guides events and tries hard to keep balance. Shiva is the destroyer; he sees rebirth through destruction. He is usually worshiped by those whose interest is in death and transformation.

Brahma the creator, Vishnu the preserver, and Shiva the destroyer: this is the eternal triad. They are the three primary gods, the primary energies that manifest themselves in existence.

Provoking these three, compelling them to manifest, is the feminine energy of *shakti*, the divine energy that gives rise to all creation. It is the complement of the male energy of the triad and is inseparable from it.

This energy of *shakti* manifests itself as a goddess. Without *shakti*, the gods are nonexistent. She becomes their consort, and her many faces represent all aspects of creation. As Sarasvati, the consort of Brahma, she is creation itself. As Lakshmi, the consort of Vishnu, she is beauty. As Parvati, the consort of Shiva, she is often referred to as Shakti and is space and time.

Shiva and Parvati are combined in this painting to symbolize the unity and inseparability of the male and female elements of existence. Hinduism attaches great importance to the dual aspect of the divine principle. From the maternal energy of fertility to the terrifying force of fierce protection, the many faces of the feminine principle are portrayed through the goddess. She is the source of all life, but within this source lies its very destruction.

BRAHMA: THE CREATOR

BRAHMA IS THE SOURCE, THE SEED, AND THE CREATOR of all things in this world. He was born of Hiranyagarbha, the golden egg or ball of fire that emerged from the primal waters. When the egg divided into two parts, heaven and earth were formed, with the blue sky between them.

Brahma with his four faces approaches Krishna with great reverence, having witnessed a great feat of his omnipresence. Brahma had set up many tests for Krishna, finally abducting a group of cows and cowherds whom Krishna then multiplied himself to replicate. This vision of each and every creature being transformed into godliness is the feat that won Brahma's heart.

Having created himself, Brahma created Sarasvati, the earth. Enchanted with her beauty, he wanted to have intercourse with her, but she, feeling playful, decided to hide from him. She became a cow, but he found her and became a bull. He made love with her, and cattle were born. Then she became a mare and he a stallion, she a ewe and he a ram. So they continued, creating all the creatures.

Brahma is often spoken of as Prajapati, the Lord of Progeny or the Abode of Man. He created not only man but the gods and demons as well. He rides upon a swan or a goose, the symbol of knowledge. In most images he appears as red or pink, the color of fire and heat. He is often portrayed as an old man with four arms and four bearded faces, which look in four directions. His hands hold the Vedas and other objects of devotion; his four faces represent the four directions, the four Vedas, the four cycles of time, and the fourfold social order of Hinduism.

In another version of the creation story it is said that Sarasvati sprang from the forehead of Brahma. As soon as he saw her, he desired her—even though she was his daughter. Sarasvati avoided the amorous attentions of this old god and kept dodging him, but whichever way she moved Brahma grew a head in that direction. As a result he grew four faces on four sides of his neck, and even a head on top of these four so that she could not escape by moving upward. But Sarasvati still eluded him. The fifth head of Brahma was eventually chopped off by Shiva, who felt that Brahma had become too obsessed with the beauty of Sarasvati.

Together Brahma and Sarasvati signify awareness or consciousness. Brahma is the source of knowledge (of both what is and what is not), and Sarasvati is existence. He is intelligence and she, the creative urge. Brahma is the primeval silence of the soul, and Sarasvati is the energy of life. Together they create the earth and all mortal beings. Brahma and Sarasvati signify the cycle of life and the cycle of the seasons. He is the light that guides the evolution of the stars, the sun, and the moon. She is earth itself. Sarasvati is the pearl of wisdom born in the shell of Brahma from a raindrop.

VISHNU: THE PRESERVER

WHEN THE DIVINE ENERGY OF BRAHMAN FIRST APPEARED, Brahma emerged from its left side. Then, in order to maintain what had been created, Vishnu emerged from the right side.

Vishnu is concerned with the world of dreams, in which things are conceived. He has no concern with the outward forms of existence, which come from Brahma; rather, he is concerned with the inner causes. He defines the principles that rule existence and destiny, as well as the actions that move the soul toward perfection.

Sleeping soundly in the coils of a serpent, with Lakshmi at his feet, Vishnu holds things together; his presence pervades existence. The name Vishnu comes from the root *visr*, which means "to spread in all directions."

Vishnu watches carefully over all the realms of existence. It is his responsibility to maintain ultimate law and order, to preserve balance and harmony. His consort, Lakshmi, is the goddess of both fortune and misfortune. She arose out of the sea of milk—the primordial cosmic ocean—at the beginning of the present age, bearing a red lotus in her hand. When she appeared, Brahma, Vishnu, and Shiva each wanted to have her for himself, but Shiva had already claimed the moon and Brahma the earth, so Vishnu won her. She has been born and reborn along with him in all of his many incarnations.

As Vishnu lies upon the boundless ocean he dreams and watches over all. From his navel a lotus arises upon which Brahma sits to live his days and nights of successive creations. After one hundred years of such days and nights, the lotus will close, and Vishnu will awake from his dream. He will then fall back into sleep and dream again.

Vishnu is associated with light, and when he walks he covers the world in three strides: on earth he moves as fire, in the sky he moves as lightning, and in the heavens he moves as the sun. He controls all that happens in the universe and has undisputed power over others. He has four arms representing the four stages of life, and his hands hold symbols of his authority. On his chest shines a brilliant gem that represents consciousness, which is embedded in the heart. To the left of the jewel is a lock of hair from his beloved Lakshmi, to whom in all their incarnations he is unfailingly devoted. He wears a garland around his throat made of five rows of flowers. These represent the five senses through which existence can be experienced. Around his hips he wears a thin yellow *dhoti*, or cloth, which represents the Vedas. His dark body shines through the thin veil just as the divine truth shines through the holy scriptures. The sacred thread that lies across his chest is made of three strands of the sacred syllable *aum*.

When he sleeps, Vishnu rests on the coiled serpent king, Sesha Naga, a symbol of immortality. He floats upon the eternal ocean of consciousness, which evokes a sense of the many destroyed universes he has seen. When he is awake, he rides in a chariot or upon the bird Garuda, who symbolizes the mind and the power of action.

With the purpose of protecting earth, Vishnu appears from time to time to set things right. In this way he tends to the balance or the integration of things. Whereas Shiva is the propensity for disintegration or death, Vishnu is the perpetuator of life.

Time

In the Hindu description of things, time is determined by a measurement of the days and nights of Brahma. Brahma sleeps and he awakens. Every time he sleeps the world falls back into its original formlessness. Each time he awakens, he again creates it. This process is continued until he completes his hundredth year. At that time he and all of existence cease to exist.

There is a beautiful image that describes the way in which the successive creations unfold. Vishnu is seen lying on a coiled snake that floats upon the cosmic ocean. As he sleeps soundly, a lotus at his navel opens and Brahma emerges to live out his life of one hundred years. Vishnu, in his sleep, watches all. As each life of Brahma comes to an end, the lotus closes and Vishnu stops dreaming.

One year in Brahma's life lasts 360 days and nights. Each day is known as one *kalpa*, and it lasts 4,320,000 human years. Each night is as long as a day, but deeply silent.

Within the creation of each *kalpa* four shorter cycles, or ages, occur. These cycles are called *yugas*. The earliest of these *yugas*, Satya Yuga, is the most perfect; it is represented by a holy bull that stands on all four legs. Moral and spiritual deterioration begins in the second age, Treta Yuga, and the bull stands on three legs. By the time the third age, Dwapara Yuga, comes around things have gotten worse; the bull stands on two legs. In the worst age, the fourth—Kali Yuga—the bull has only one leg upon which to stand.

The *yugas* vary in length, the first being the longest.

Satya Yuga	1.7 million earthly years
Treta Yuga	1.3 million earthly years
Dwapara Yuga	0.9 million earthly years
Kali Yuga	0.4 million earthly years

The present Kali Yuga dawned about 3000 B.C.E. This is the age we are in. According to this understanding of things, there have been three *yugas* before ours in this particular creation. There are several hundred thousand years still to come before it ends.

Passage of the Yugas

During the passage of the *yugas* there is a slow and irreversible deterioration of the cosmic order or spiritual energy of things. In the cycles of the *yugas*, goodness vanishes by degrees from the world, and humans become filled with lust and evil. When the world has deteriorated beyond any salvation, it is destroyed by Shiva.

In each of the four *yugas*, imbalances are created by a variety of adverse conditions. They are set right by different incarnations of Vishnu, who appears in several forms in order to hold the universe together.

SHIVA: THE DESTROYER

ALL THAT HAS A BEGINNING MUST HAVE AN END. All that is born must die. All that exists must cease to exist. The universal power of destruction in which all existence ends and from which it rises again is known as Shiva, the Lord of Sleep.

Nothing in our existence can escape the process of destruction and death, for creation depends upon it. Shiva is the link between lives (death) and between moments (eternity). He is known as the fathomless abyss.

In the Mahabharata, Shiva is given 1,008 names describing his different aspects. Rudra, the Lord of Tears, represents the fierce, active mode of destruction; it is in this form that Shiva appears in the Vedas, as a powerful but dangerous god. He is the howling of storms, the father of the wind, and sometimes the god of fire. In the Rig Veda he presides over sacrifice and is spoken of as the Lord of Songs. He is also described as the Great Fear, the upraised thunderbolt whose anger makes even the gods afraid. Shiva is the Lord of Fire and Bhairava the Terrible—the destroyer who takes pleasure in destruction for its own sake. Shiva is Hara the Remover, or Death. He is disease and he is the remover of pain. Shiva is often pictured asleep, for when beings are tired of action, of pain and pleasure, they seek the rest of dreamless sleep, where they can enter into Shiva, the Abode of Joy.

One day Parvati, the beautiful consort of Shiva, crept behind him and playfully placed her hands over his eyes. Suddenly darkness engulfed the whole world and all beings trembled in great fear, for the eyes of Shiva had closed. Within a

Shiva (sitting with legs crossed in the lotus position) has been worshipped as long as images have been made. He is the great ascetic who preserves the world through meditation, and as such the gods worship him. With many faces, he looks in all directions. With many arms he cares for everything. The garland of skulls that hangs around his neck represents the transient nature of all things.

Vishnu and the sun-bird Garuda pay an unexpected visit to Shiva. The snake, which had been sitting on his loins, darts into an anthill at the sight of the bird. Parvati tears a strip from her patchwork scarf and hands it to Shiva as she shyly averts her eyes. Vishnu looks on with amusement.

moment, a massive tongue of flame leapt from the forehead of Shiva and a third eye appeared to give light to the world. This, Shiva's eye of fire, is the eye of higher perception. It normally looks inward, but when directed outward, it burns all that appears before it. With a glance of the third eye the gods and all created beings are destroyed each time the universe ends.

Shiva is pictured as white in color, for he is the embodiment of enlightenment. He has three eyes, representing the sun, the moon, and fire, the three sources of light that illuminate the earth. Through his eyes, Shiva can see past, present, and future. On his head he wears the moon; it is *soma*, the elixir of life, the intoxicating ambrosia of the divinities. The river Ganges, which purifies all things, flows from his crown.

Shiva wears a tiger skin, denoting his victory over every force. He has four arms, a sign of mastery over the elements, and in his hands he holds various tools of destruction. Around his neck he wears a snake, the symbol of the dormant energy of *kundalini*, the energy that rises with awareness, as well as a garland of skulls, which represents the perpetual appearance and disappearance of the human race.

Nandi, the bull upon which Shiva rides, is an embodiment of justice and virtue. He also represents the sexual impulse, which can be used for the conquest of the self. Worshipers of Shiva touch the testicles of Nandi as they enter a temple, for they are the source of life.

Surabhi, foremother of all cows, emerged from the primeval ocean of milk to bless the world with plenty. Here she approaches Vishnu to beg him to incarnate and rid the world of demons. Around the perfect circle of dream-vision stand Brahma with his four heads, Shiva in a tiger skin, an incarnation of blue-skinned Vishnu, and Indra, who is covered in peacock eyes.

Ten Incarnations
of Vishnu

OVER THE CENTURIES, MANY GODS OF THE HINDU PANTHEON have become identified with Vishnu, appearing not as manifestations but as incarnations. Whenever the world has needed help in its evolution or has been in danger of being overcome by evil, Vishnu has been called upon. His response always takes form in the creation of another god.

Reaching far back in time to ages of mankind that precede our own, the history of the present creation is spanned by nine significant incarnations of Vishnu, with one still to come. The stories of these incarnations serve as a background to Hinduism and also to the world. They include the fable of the flood that spread throughout the Middle East and stories of the battles and heroes of India.

Some of Vishnu's incarnations have inspired great epics. Rama, of the Ramayana, and Krishna, of the Mahabharata, have taken their places alongside Shiva and Vishnu in the hearts of Hindus, and their renown has spread far beyond the shores of their homeland.

The stories that unfold in the following pages are but the smallest taste of the complex tales that are told regarding Vishnu's incarnations. Underlying these stories is the phenomenon of evil. The significance of evil in the Hindu view of things is that it is ultimately helpful, for evil creates the necessary friction that results in higher understanding. In no way does this absolve those who engage in evil acts; rather, it serves as the basis for compassionate understanding and an ever more enlightened approach to dealing with it.

As the day of Brahma draws to a close and values inevitably deteriorate, Vishnu's incarnations become more spiritual, for as the pull of evil becomes stronger the compensating energy must be more pronounced. At the same time the forms of Vishnu become successively more human, creating an enduring impression of the close relationship between God and being.

The Story of Jaya and Vijaya

The story of Vishnu's incarnations begins as Brahma awakens. During his sleep, all of existence has been drowned in the cosmic ocean. Vishnu's first tasks involve helping to get things started again. The story of Jaya and Vijaya sets the scene for many lives to come.

Two brothers, Jaya and Vijaya, had been appointed doorkeepers of heaven. One day four saints came to pay homage to the gods, and the brothers, who had become very arrogant, tried to stop them. The saints grew angry and cursed Jaya and Vijaya: "You are so lucky to have been appointed doorkeepers, and yet you are so terribly arrogant. Go! Wander in the world below and learn about humility."

The two doorkeepers were shocked at this. Trembling with regret, they prayed to Vishnu, who told them, "These men have great spiritual powers. Their words will come true. I must see to it. You will go to the lands below earth and come back when you have learned about humility."

So it was that Jaya and Vijaya fell from heaven to be born as twin *rakshasas*, or demons in the underworld. In the three ages that followed they became enemies of God and of the way to God. They struggled against good and were overcome, and thus they learned their lesson.

Their first incarnation was in the Satya Yuga. Named Hiranyakasipu and Hiranyaksha, the brothers were killed by Varaha and Narasimha, two of Vishnu's incarnations. In the Treta Yuga, they were born as Ravana and Kumbhakarna and were killed by Rama. Finally, in the Dwapara Yuga they were born as Shishupala and Dantavakra. When Krishna killed them he freed them from the curse.

The birth of Hiranyakasipu and Hiranyaksha starts the story of Vishnu's first incarnation. The gods trembled with fear when they were born, for they were horribly ferocious and very powerful. The younger of the two, Hiranyaksha, was the stronger. He devised a plan to attack the kingdom of the gods. As he approached, the gods were stricken with fear. There was a terrible battle in which Hiranyaksha tried to seize the goddess Earth, but in the confusion of the battle, Earth fell into the ocean. The gods prayed for help.

VARAHA: THE BOAR
The First Incarnation of Vishnu

CHASING AFTER EARTH, HIRANYAKSHA DIVED into the water and met Varuna, the Lord of the Ocean, who stood in his way. Hiranyaksha called for a fight, but Varuna answered, "O great hero, I am a simple hermit. I do not wish to fight. Besides, who can fight with you and not lose? Only Vishnu himself can do that."

As Varuna spoke, a very small boar shot out from one of Brahma's nostrils and, as the gods looked on, began to grow. The boar grew and grew until he was the size of a mountain. The boar was Varaha, an incarnation of Vishnu.

Varaha dived deep into the ocean and picked up the drowning Earth. He placed her on his tusks and carried her toward the surface so that Brahma might breathe life back into her.

Hiranyaksha, seeing the boar, realized in a moment that he must be Vishnu. Arrogantly he cried out, "Foolish boar, leave Earth where she is and go away. If you want her, you will have to fight me for her." So saying he moved to stop Varaha. Varaha took no notice of him and continued to rise to the surface.

Hiranyaksha called out again, "Coward! Come and fight against me."

With this Varaha put Earth aside, saying to Hiranyaksha, "These words of empty pride will lead you right into the jaws of death." A dreadful fight ensued. Hours later, the battle finally ended when the divine boar struck a stunning blow on Hiranyaksha's cheek. The blow was so terrible that Hiranyaksha fell to the ground and died.

Varaha then picked up Earth and placed her in her rightful place.

With Earth safely held on his tusks, Varaha defeats the evil Hiranyaksha. In some versions of the story, plants and animals were breeding upon Earth in such profusion that she could not bear the burden and fell into the Underworld. Vishnu then descended into the dark waters and pushed Earth to the surface, setting her amidst the oceans in such a way that she could never fall down again.

KURMA: THE TORTOISE
The Second Incarnation of Vishnu

DURING THE FLOOD AT THE BEGINNING of the present *kalpa*, the gods lost their immortality. Each time Brahma falls asleep this happens. They appealed to Vishnu for help. He told them that they must move Mount Mandara to the ocean. With it they could churn the water into butter and make an ambrosia that would bring the gods immortality again. But, Vishnu said, they would need the help of the demons.

So the gods and *devas* (those who inhabit the realm between mortals and gods) convinced the demons to help. Together they all went to Mount Mandara. Digging up the mountain and dragging it to the ocean was a difficult job, and many lives were lost. Finally they succeeded. The mountain was in the water, bound with Vasuki, the King of Snakes. The gods, *devas*, and demons began the work of churning, but as they did so, the mountain began to slide into the sea.

Vishnu appeared as Kurma, in the form of a tortoise. He swam to the bottom of the sea and placed himself beneath the mountain to hold it in place. The churning began again. As the ocean began to turn, many of the things of divine value that had been lost in the flood reappeared. These included Kaustubha, the most precious stone; Surabhi, the cow of abundance; Varuni, the goddess of wine; Parijata, the celestial tree that fulfils every desire; Lakshmi, who became the consort of Vishnu; Chandra, the moon, which was taken by Shiva and placed on his head; and finally Dhanvantari, the physician of the gods. Dhanvantari held in his hands a pot with the precious ambrosia.

The story of Kurma is based upon an early creation myth. As the the gods churned the ocean, the fumes of a terrible poison arose from the waters. Vishnu consumed this poison and retained it in his throat. This event is celebrated by Hindus just before sunset.

The small squares to the left and right of Vishnu's head represent the first written texts of the sacred Vedas. This vast complex of sacred teachings is divided into four parts: the Veda of poetry, of songs, of sacrificial texts, and of the mystical fire ceremony.

The demons immediately pounced upon him and stole the pot of ambrosia. A fierce battle broke out. To put an end to the battle, Vishnu rose out of the ocean in the shape of a beautiful maiden. She appealed to the demons to hand over the ambrosia, saying that she wanted to serve it to them. She told everyone to sit in two rows—the gods and *devas* on one side, the demons on the other—and proceeded to serve them all. To the demons she gave an intoxicating liquor and to the gods and *devas* she gave the ambrosia that made them immortal once again.

MATSYA: THE FISH
The Third Incarnation of Vishnu

DURING THE PERIOD OF TIME BETWEEN THE CREATION of our humanity and the one that preceded it, the Vedas had been stolen from the sleeping Brahma and thrown into the ocean. As work on our present humanity began, it became necessary to retrieve them in order to instruct humans in their work. Vishnu was therefore appointed to bring the Vedas up from the deep.

Manu, the founder of present-day humanity, was handed a jug of water with which to bathe. Gazing into the jug he saw a fish, which jumped into his hand and asked for protection, saying, "Keep me; I will save you from the flood that will sweep away all the creatures of the earth." So Manu kept the fish.

Day by day, the fish grew larger, and Manu had to move him into ever larger vessels of water. Finally nothing but the ocean could hold him. At this point, Manu recognized Vishnu in the fish and understood that he must prepare for an approaching flood. He built a ship and placed upon it all the plants and animals of the earth.

Matsya the fish, having grown to an enormous size, swam toward the ship, which Manu then fastened to Matsya's horn. Thus Manu was guided to safety when the waters subsided.

During the time of the flood, Matsya battled with the terrible demon who had stolen the Vedas. He succeeded in winning the battle, and once Manu was back on dry land, Matsya gave the Vedas to Manu and taught him the principles of knowledge that should guide the human race.

NARASIMHA: THE MAN-LION
The Fourth Incarnation of Vishnu

AT HIRANYAKSHA'S DEATH AT THE HANDS of Varaha, his wife was overcome with grief. Hiranyakasipu, Hiranyaksha's elder brother, tried to console her by telling her that everyone has to die: "Do not weep. My brother fought and died like a hero." But even as he tried to console her, sorrow burned in his heart like fire and his blood boiled with hatred for Vishnu. He called together the generals of his army and told them to give the devotees of Vishnu as much trouble as they could; so they burned the cities and razed the temples to the ground.

Meanwhile Hiranyakasipu hatched a plan. He went to the top of a mountain and began a great meditation. He stood on one toe with his arms raised straight up and his eyes looking at the sky. In this stance he offered a prayer to Brahma. Flames rose from his body and enveloped the entire universe. Rivers and oceans boiled. The earth shook. Fire spread on all sides, and even the gods were filled with fear. They prayed to Brahma to save them. So Brahma appeared before Hiranyakasipu and said to him, "Hiranyakasipu, I am pleased with your devotion. Ask for whatever you desire."

Hiranyakasipu replied, "I want immortality. I want to be free of death by man or animal; I want to be free of death from either inside or outside my house; I want to be free of death in the day or at night."

While Hiranyakasipu was meditating, a son named Prahlada was born to him—a son who from his birth was inspired with love and devotion to Vishnu.

When Hiranyakasipu returned to his kingdom, he called his son to him and kissed him gently. Setting him on his knee, Hiranyakasipu asked the boy, "Well, child, tell me what you have learned from your teachers." Prahlada replied with a question that had been gnawing at him for some time: "Since we are all sparks of one glowing fire, who then is an enemy and who a friend?"

"What do you mean, my son? Enemy? Is there someone you fear?"

"Fear?" replied Prahlada. "No. I am not afraid at all, for I know that Vishnu is present everywhere in the world."

With the mention of the name Vishnu, Hiranyakasipu felt as if hot lead had been poured into his heart. Vishnu was his enemy, and his own son was speaking of the god with devotion.

In a fury he jumped up. "What do you mean you are not afraid? If you think you are not afraid, you are gravely mistaken," he cried, and he called upon one of his soldiers to strike Prahlada with the sharp point of a lance. But the point would not pierce the boy's body. Not a hair was hurt. He had his son trampled by an elephant but nothing happened. He ordered him to be thrown into the river, but Prahlada joyously floated on the water, repeating the sacred names of Vishnu. Prahlada was given poison; but his devotion changed it into nectar. The demonking's servants pushed him from the ledge of a mountain rock, but he fell like a light flower. Thrown into fire, he glowed. Rain, wind, snow, and sun—nothing could hurt Prahlada in the least.

"You! The three worlds tremble at my glance, but you, my son, you dare to confront me?" Hiranyakasipu angrily asked his son. "I am the lord of all the worlds, the only master! Is there another? If so, where is he? Show him to me."

Vishnu emerges from a pillar, incarnated as the man-lion Narasimha. Metaphorically, the man-lion represents the strength and courage needed to destroy ignorance.

"He is everywhere," replied the young Prahlada.

The king could no longer control himself. He drew his sword and pounced upon the little boy. With this there was a deafening noise, as if the universe had split in two; even Hiranyakasipu was startled.

As everyone watched, the pillar he was standing next to split into two and Vishnu appeared in the form of Narasimha, with the head of a lion and the body of a man.

Hiranyakasipu was a man of extraordinary strength, but he could do nothing against Narasimha, who caught him like a snake seizing a mouse and placed him in his lap. Then Narasimha dug his nails deep into the body of Hiranyakasipu and tore it open. He took out the entrails and put them around his neck.

At this, Hiranyakasipu's bodyguards sprang to action, but they were all crushed with a single blow. Narasimha sat on the throne of Hiranyakasipu, and Prahlada approached and touched his feet in deep devotion.

Narasimha explained to Prahlada that his father had won blessings of immortality from Brahma through a devious trick. Narasimha had respected the promises of Brahma. "It is twilight now," he said, "which is neither day nor night; the place of his death is neither inside the house nor outside it, but on the lap of God; he was killed by neither man nor animal but by Vishnu in the form of Narasimha, who is half man, half lion."

Then Vishnu told Prahlada that he was pleased and set him to rule over the kingdoms of earth and the underworld for some time. "Live happily. Do only what is right and just, so that all men will be happy."

VAMANA: THE DWARF
The Fifth Incarnation of Vishnu

BALI, THE GRANDSON OF PRAHLADA, later became king of earth and ruler of the underworld. He was generous and wise. Because of his exceptional abilities, Brahma gave him power over all the worlds—including the world of the gods. With this, the gods naturally felt humiliated.

Vishnu came to their assistance once again, this time by appearing as a dwarf. He descended to earth and appeared before Bali in the hall where a powerful ritual of sacrifice was being performed. The ritual included the ceremonial pouring of water from golden vessels. One such vessel was in the hands of Bali, who was being helped by his wife. The dwarf Vamana entered the hall just as the water was to be poured and humbly approached Bali. Bali, in the spirit of the ceremony, asked the dwarf to participate by making a request, to which the humble dwarf replied that all he wanted was as much land as could be measured in three steps.

Bali gave his consent. Before their very eyes, Vamana grew to such dimensions that with his first step he covered the celestial world and with the second, the earthly. At this the dwarf stopped, having restored to the gods their power over the celestial and the earthly worlds. The underworld he left to the demons, for it belongs to them.

This painting captures Vishnu as Vamana the dwarf moments before he grows to unfathomable dimensions. The three worlds that are conquered by Vishnu's subsequent giant steps represent the sphere of desire, the sphere of desirelessness, and the sphere of formlessness.

PARASHURAMA: RAMA WITH AN AX
The Sixth Incarnation of Vishnu

IN HIS SIXTH INCARNATION, VISHNU BEGAN to take on the form of a full-grown man, a hero. His later incarnations spanned the complete lifetime of a human being, and the detailed stories surrounding these incarnations deal with subtleties of the complex moral issues of right and wrong and with spiritual issues of karma, devotion, and attachment.

The incarnation of Vishnu as Parashurama, or Rama with an Ax, took place after a social revolution wherein the kings and merchants of the earth had wrestled leadership from the *rishis*, or sages. One of the greatest dangers that has ever menaced society, say the ancient teachings, is this type of revolt, for it is the first step in the uncontrolled rule of kings and merchants.

Sometime after the revolt, the king learned of a sage named Jamadagnya who possessed a sacred cow that could grant wishes. The king wanted this cow at any price and had it stolen. Parashurama, the son of Jamadagnya, killed the king, whose son avenged the king's death by killing Parashurama's father. This resulted in a terrible war between Parashurama and the followers of the king. After twenty-one battles, Parashurama cleared the earth of these followers and reestablished as rulers the sons of the ancient kings, who had been hidden by the sages.

Vishnu is thought to have had many minor incarnations in which he brought to the world such gifts as the message of divine love and devotion, the Tantras, the medical sciences, and music. In each of these incarnations, he destroyed evil demons that plagued mankind in order to establish those aspects of life that support the transformation of the human soul.

RAMA: HERO OF THE RAMAYANA
The Seventh Incarnation of Vishnu

THE STORY OF RAMA, THE SEVENTH INCARNATION of Vishnu, has become the subject of the epic poem the Ramayana. A story is told of its author, the ancient poet Valmiki. Valmiki was walking along the banks of a river one day, contemplating the story of Rama. Glancing up, he noticed two lovebirds; as he looked on, the male was killed by a hunter. The female bird cried out in grief, and Valmiki, stirred by her cries, exclaimed, "O hunter, will you ever find rest? For you have killed a small bird in the midst of his love."

These words and the feeling that poured from Valmiki's heart were spoken spontaneously in the form of a musical verse of a particular meter. At the sound of it, Brahma appeared before Valmiki and told him to sing the story of Rama in the rhythm of the verse he had just sung, saying, "As long as this world endures, as long as the stars shine in heaven, so long will this song spread among men."

Valmiki went on to compose the twenty-four thousand verses that make up the Ramayana, the incredible saga that is said to contain the essence of all Vedas and all sacred scriptures. The Ramayana is one of Hinduism's great treasures, a reservoir of tales that are told over and over. The epic concerns Rama, who is respected among Hindus and non-Hindus as the embodiment of righteousness.

Toward the end of the Treta Yuga (the second age) there was a demon-king named Ravana who lived in Sri Lanka. Concerned about retribution from the gods, he had pleased Brahma by austere penances, and Brahma had made him invulnerable to the gods.

Devotion to Rama and Hanuman (the monkey god, upper left) is widespread among Hindus. Vishnu's incarnation as Rama helped develop the quality of truth as a virtue in humanity. The word *rama* means "charming," and it is chanted as one of Hinduism's basic mantras.

In an episode of the Ramayana, Rama helped Valin, the rightful king of the monkey kingdom, to regain his throne. In a test of his extraordinary abilities, he shot a single arrow through seven trees.

Thus fortified, Ravana began his reign of terror and misuse of power. The gods approached Brahma to relieve them of the looming danger and deliver the people from their sufferings. Brahma disclosed to them that Ravana, in his pride, had thought that only gods could overpower him and had not included man among those he was protected against. The gods then approached Vishnu, who promised to descend to earth incarnated as a man.

Rama was born in Ayodhya as the eldest son of King Dasaratha. He had one brother and two half brothers, all of whom were deeply devoted to one another. Rama's brother Lakshmana was especially devoted to him.

King Dasaratha, about to die, chose Rama as his heir. However, his wife demanded that he appoint a younger son, Bharata, as king and that he banish Rama to the forest for fourteen years. The king reluctantly acquiesced, and Rama went to the forest to live as a hermit with his beautiful wife, Sita, and his brother Lakshmana.

In the forest they met a demoness who fell in love with Rama. When Rama refused her advances she fled to her brother, Ravana; after hearing of Sita's beauty, Ravana decided that he must have her. Disguised as a wandering ascetic, Ravana went to the forest to find Sita, and while Rama and Lakshmana were distracted he carried her off.

Distraught, Rama and his brother enlisted the services of Hanuman, the monkey god, to help find Sita. Hanuman was able to make himself larger or smaller at will, and so he took a giant step to the island of Lanka and found her.

After a long battle, Rama killed Ravana. Together with Sita, Lakshmana, and Hanuman, he returned to Ayodhya to regain his kingdom. His people, however, did not receive Sita wholeheartedly, questioning her chastity. Rama asked Sita to undergo a fire test, to which she agreed. Having proved her chastity, she was once again rejoined with Rama, only to be ultimately abandoned by him in a final display of duty.

On the night he learned of her pregnancy, Rama also learned that among his people an attitude had grown that condoned unfaithfulness between a man and his wife. Torn by his love, Rama was obliged to honor his promise to help humanity by sending Sita away, for he understood that his people would never respect him unless he proved to them that his love for them surpassed even his love for his wife. The sacrifice caused great sorrow, but Rama's righteousness was proven. His people learned to trust in good again, and Rama ruled for eleven thousand years. Finally, when he left the world and returned to the eternal realm, he and Sita were reunited.

KRISHNA: HERDSMAN AND FLUTIST
The Eighth Incarnation of Vishnu

TOWARD THE END OF THE THIRD STAGE of the Dwapara Yuga (the third age), or just before our present age, Vishnu returned to earth incarnated as Krishna, the embodiment of love and of the divine joy that destroys all pain.

The story of Krishna has been immortalized in the Mahabharata, another of the great epics in world literature. For many, the most important part of the long epic is the Bhagavad Gita, which contains Krishna's instructions to the warrior Arjuna just before the beginning of the eighteen-day battle whose dramatic events are the focal point of the epic.

The Bhagavad Gita, or "Song of the Exalted One," is considered to be the "gospel" of Hinduism. In it Krishna promises to the descendants of Bharata that whenever and wherever there is a decline in religious practice and a predominant

During his incarnation as Rama, Vishnu wandered into a forest and rescued some sages from a demon. His beauty was such that the sages grew sick with the longing to be near him and Vishnu promised them that he would return in another incarnation and that the sages would then become cowherdesses and would make endless love with him.

rise of those opposed to religion, he will descend to deliver the pious, annihilate evil, and reestablish the principles of religion. Krishna is believed to appear millennium after millennium for this purpose.

Setting the scene for the incarnation of Krishna was a battle between the demons and the gods. When the demons were defeated, they decided to attack earth, and they invaded our realm by discreetly taking birth as princes in powerful royal families.

Seeing earth overrun by the militaristic activities of these kingly demons, the gods sought Vishnu's intervention. As Krishna he was born to Devaki, who had been imprisoned by the wicked ruler Kamsa after a sage predicted that her eighth child would slay him. One by one, six sons were killed. The last two babes were exchanged with children from nearby farms, and Krishna, the youngest, grew up as a cowherd. There are numerous legends of his childhood.

One day a well-dressed woman named Gokula approached the newborn Krishna and attempted to feed him at her breast. The woman had in fact been sent by Kamsa to kill Krishna with her poisonous milk, but Krishna smilingly sucked the milk from her breast and killed her by sucking out her life.

Fear of further troubles with Kamsa prompted the family to move to Vrindavan, a nearby township, where Krishna and his friends grew up. The woods, the banks of the river, the valleys, and the fields echoed with their loud shouts and gay laughter. Krishna won the love of everyone and proved himself a born leader. He enchanted many cowgirls—of whom Radha was

One rainy season the townspeople were making preparations to worship Indra, the god of rains. Krishna felt it was not Indra but a nearby hill that caused the rains, and he suggested that they should worship the hill. Indra was furious at this and decided to punish them. The sky opened up and the rains came down in torrents. The townspeople were terrified, but Krishna lifted up the hill and held it like an umbrella over them.

his favorite—with the music of his flute and danced with them in the moonlight.

As Krishna grew older he proved to be as gifted in battle as he was in pleasure. He outsmarted and killed the wicked Kamsa with his own hands. One famous battle led to another as one complex intrigue gave rise to another, and Krishna lived out the rest of his life restoring the virtuous to their rightful places. By the time he reached the end of his life, evil had completely disappeared.

BUDDHA: THE ENLIGHTENED ONE
The Ninth Incarnation of Vishnu

CALM AND GRACEFUL IN APPEARANCE, Buddha, the ninth incarnation of Vishnu, appeared at the start of the present age. Seeing that many humans no longer regarded the ancient scriptures as valuable, Vishnu decided to preach a false religion and in this way separate the true believers from the false.

The teachings of Buddhism, which grew out of Vishnu's incarnation as Buddha, have become one of the world's great religions, so from our perspective it is difficult to tell what is a false religion and what is true, and which believers have been saved. During his life and for several hundred years thereafter, Buddha was disavowed by Hindus, for in their eyes the religiousness he taught was false. Nonetheless, the power of this great incarnation of Vishnu remains with us, inspiring many people, who have found the Buddhist techniques of meditation to be of enormous help in creating balance in life.

Gautama Buddha, or Siddhartha, was born twenty-five hundred years ago into the Gautama

Believing that the teachings of Gautama Buddha had turned people away from the Vedas, Hindu priests chased his followers out of India and destroyed any art that depicted him. The painting at the right is one of the very few Hindu images of Buddha that remain.

clan in northern India. Although Hindus and Buddhists disagree on many of the accounts of what has come to pass, on the legends of his birth they concur.

Vishnu took the form of a white six-tusked elephant and, when the time was right, entered the body of Queen Mayadevi through the right side of her rib cage. Mayadevi carried the child in her womb for ten months. One day while strolling in her garden, she felt that the birth was imminent. She reached up to grasp at the branch of a tree and yawned. Immediately, amid an aura of light, the child was born from under her right arm. He walked seven steps in each direction and the earth shook in homage. The child was named Siddhartha.

Grown up and married, Siddhartha was riding through a village one day when, in a dreamlike state, he realized that the inevitable outcome of life is disease and death. Back in his father's palace, he dressed in rags, then left his family in the middle of the night and went in search of that which does not die. Hoping to glean a sense of what he sought from Hindu sages, he listened to them all. But their words were meaningless to him. He tried in every way to reach the ecstatic states they talked of, and every attempt failed. Exhausted after several years of the most intense asceticism, he stopped trying and suddenly realized nirvana.

In an enlightened state, Buddha began to roam the country, teaching a new spirituality. Although he gathered thousands of disciples, many of whom were transformed in his presence, Hindu priests did not accept him. What he taught undermined their own authority. Within a few years of his death, Hindu priests forced the followers of the Buddhist teachings to flee India.

The teachings of Buddha became the basis for a great revolution in spirituality that has persisted for three thousand years. It is a spirituality that encourages the seeker to search for emptiness within, to discover their own Buddha-nature.

Still alive and continuing to influence our generations, the wisdom of Buddha is withstanding the test of time, teaching messages of human transformation that are the keys to peace and compassion.

For many, Buddha-nature is neither Hindu nor Buddhist. It does not belong to any creed or religion, for it is a state in which doctrines and laws, beliefs and morals have no relevance. It is an inner state of peace and has nothing to do with outer appearance. Buddhists believe that true religiousness is not colored by belief in any particular doctrine. Nirvana is a state of complete freedom.

KALKI: JUDGE AND SAVIOR
The Tenth and Last Incarnation of Vishnu

KALKI IS AN INCARNATION OF THE FUTURE who will appear at the end of the present era. He is represented both as the judge who will punish evil and as the savior of the righteous. Kalki is usually depicted with a white horse, representing the indestructible, the hidden nature of things.

It is understood by Hindus that the more difficult *yugas* would see more powerful incarnations of Vishnu. Each passing age demands a more potent incarnation in order to balance the energies and redeem the world. It is said that in the Kali Yuga (the present age), moral conditions will reach their nadir and will require the most potent incarnation of all to restore order in the world. That incarnation is believed to be Kalki.

The Mahabharata says that in a certain village called Shambal, a son will be born into the priestly class of India that are known as Brahmans, in the house of a man named Vishnuyasha. This boy's name will be Kalki. He will be extremely

When he arrives, Kalki will overcome the terrible darkness that will have descended upon the world. He will resolve the fear and greed that blind human beings and usher in a period of awakening and great peace. Kalki's horse is white—the color that unites all colors and represents true virtue. In his hand, Kalki carries the flaming sword of truth that destroys all ignorance.

powerful, intelligent, and valiant. Collecting a huge army of warriors, he will go about setting righteous order back in the world. He will not only reestablish the rule of *dharma* but will also herald the advent of the Golden Age, or the Satya Yuga of the next cycle of time.

Dharma is a term used to refer to true nature, or that which knows itself as God. True nature is not complicated by desires or by longing for what is not. The rule of *dharma*, once it is reestablished, will bring about peace and prosperity. Fear and greed will disappear. Life will be transformed as human beings are transformed. This is the gift of the gods.

The Pantheon of Hindu Gods

THIS BOOK WOULD NOT BE COMPLETE without a look at some of the many gods and goddesses that support the triad of Brahma, Vishnu, and Shiva.

The gods of Hinduism have evolved through many centuries of storytelling. Naturally, they reflect developing beliefs as well as the changing issues that beset a people. Just as great floods and wars are the basis for well-known stories, so too are the dramatic shifts brought on by foreign invaders and the introduction of new ideas that arise from the exchanges of trade and travel. As the world around them continued to change, so too did the stories and personalities of the Hindu gods.

There is no quintessential description of the particular gods of Hinduism. Different scriptures

Vishnu and Lakshmi are riding upon Garuda, king of the birds and archenemy of the serpents. Garuda also represents the words of the Vedas, magic words on whose wings humans can be transported from one world into another.

portray them differently, and storytellers continue to embellish their tales. However, like wildflowers in a field, they can be randomly picked and called upon, for, like flowers, each has a particular scent, or quality. The Hindu gods are not the insubstantial idols of religious rites; they are living aspects of human nature that are personified in order to enlighten, to inspire, and to teach.

Krishna wrestles with the bull-demon Arishta, who shattered the tranquil existence of Vrindavan by fouling the earth and terrorizing the helpless people with a terrible noise. Krishna wrenches a horn from the beast with which he then impales him.

In the pages that follow, remember that the stories you read are about the struggle to be free. The price of freedom is determined by karma—our actions. If we battle with our demons, like the gods we will be free. While it is true that the stories of the Hindu gods seem to dwell on an eternal procession of battles, it is also true that if they were not fighting on our behalf, our world would long ago have dissolved into the terrible chaos of ignorance and fear.

DURGA
The Invincible

DURGA IS A FIERCE FORM OF THE MOTHER GODDESS. According to a legend, the gods could not defeat the buffalo demon, Mahisha, who was threatening the existence of the universe. They begged Shiva for his assistance, so Shiva advised all the gods to release their *shakti* energy. The energy that was thus released fused together in a blinding light, and there arose a magnificent, fully grown goddess with many arms who was as beautiful as she was deadly. The gods called her Durga, the Invincible One, and they armed her with all their weapons. Durga rode to the top of a mountain on a lion. In a bloody battle, she defeated Mahisha and his army of demons and thus saved the world.

Originally Durga was seen as the embodiment of the natural forces that both grant life and take it away. As such, she nourishes with the ingenuity and unfailing dedication of nature and protects with a vengeance.

She is also known as the Unfathomable One, for she destroys ignorance. In exchange for this she demands a sacrifice; in some stories, this sacrifice involves a human life.

Durga is the power of realization and the destroyer of the world of illusion. She is sometimes known as Beyond-Reach and in this aspect is another manifestation of the consort of Shiva. The lion she rides upon depicts courage.

Energy, or *shakti*, is pictured by Hindus as female. It arises out of the tension between opposites and gives rise to motion and to the manifest world. That which is divine is nothing more than an abundance of energy.

GANESHA
Remover of Obstacles

PROBABLY THE MOST POPULAR GOD in all of India is Ganesha, god of wisdom and patron of sciences, arts, and creative activities. With a figure made up of both man and elephant, he represents the microcosm and the macrocosm. The elephant is a symbol of the human potential to become enlightened. The rat he rides upon is able to pass anywhere.

Ganesha is the son of Shiva and Parvati. Parvati entreated Shiva to beget her a son, but Shiva would hear nothing of it. He had no desire, he said, to be a householder, for such a state is troublesome. Seeing Parvati's distress at this, Shiva pulled a thread from the dress she wore and made a son from it. Parvati suckled the babe at her breast, and he came to life. As he sucked at her milk he smiled, and Parvati, pleased, handed the son to Shiva. Shiva was surprised that Parvati had breathed life into a child made of fabric and warned her that the birth of the child was inauspicious. As he spoke, the child's head fell to the ground.

Parvati was overcome with grief as Shiva tried unsuccessfully to put the head back on the child's body. Suddenly a voice came from the sky and said that the head of someone facing north would stick to the child. Shiva sent Nandi, the bull upon which he rides, to find such a person. Nandi soon found Indra's elephant Airavata lying with his head facing north. He began to cut it off. Indra tried to stop him but Nandi was successful, although one of the tusks was broken in the struggle. Nandi took the elephant head to Shiva, who placed it upon the child. Thus Ganesha was born. The gods celebrated the birth and Parvati was pleased.

Ganesha is the Remover of Obstacles and is worshipped at the beginning of every undertaking and every journey. Here he is visited by Sarasvati, who serves with him as a patron to the arts.

HANUMAN
Companion of Rama

HANUMAN, THE WELL-KNOWN MONKEY GOD, can be seen in temples throughout India, most often in a devotional posture before images of Rama and Sita. He is considered to be a god of power and strength who remained celibate throughout his life. As the greatest devotee of Rama, he is cherished as a symbol of the emotional attitude of a servant to the master.

Hanuman is the son of Vayu, the Lord of Winds, and Arijana, a female monkey whom Vayu had seduced. When only ten years old, Hanuman could lift hills that were sixteen or twenty miles in circumference and could throw them like stones.

When quite young Hanuman saw the rising sun and thought it to be a ripe fruit. He jumped up and, seizing the sun, put it in his mouth. Fearing that if he swallowed the sun the whole world would perish, all the gods and goddesses prayed to him to spit out the sun. Hanuman agreed, and the world was saved from complete darkness.

On another occasion a female monster tried to swallow him. Hanuman expanded his body, but the monster continued to stretch her mouth, until it was one hundred leagues wide. Suddenly Hanuman shrank his body and within seconds became thumb-sized. Taking the demon by surprise, he darted forward and came out through her right ear.

One of the great services of Hanuman was to fly to the Himalayas to bring herbs with which to cure Rama and his brother when they had been mortally wounded. Hanuman's magic healing powers are invoked in times of great duress or sickness.

INDRA
Chief of the Heavens

INDRA IS THE GOD OF THE HEAVENS and the chief of the senses. He is terribly jealous. Whenever anyone is on the verge of enlightenment, Indra sends down *apsaras*, visions of beautiful women, to distract them.

The parents of Indra were the sky god and the earth goddess. He is the god of thunder and storms and is the greatest of all warriors, defending both gods and mankind against the forces of evil. He is the ruler of the atmosphere, and the weather is at his command.

Indra is worshiped as a fertility god who brings rain. He is also a great drinker of *soma*, the elixir of the gods—sometimes to gather strength for battle, but more often to get drunk. He rides either in a chariot or upon his great white elephant Airavata, who resembles a sacred mountain.

In one of Indra's notable exploits he battled with the mighty dragon Vritra, who had stolen all the water in the world for himself. Upon hearing what had happened, Indra vowed to get back the life-giving liquid. Before going to meet Vritra he consumed enormous amounts of *soma*. He then smashed through Vritra's ninety-nine fortresses and, after a long battle, split him open. As he did so, water again fell from the skies, and Indra became a hero to all.

Indra was the supreme deity of very early Hindus. He consumed vast quantities of the intoxicating juice of the *soma* plant that is often referred to as the "wine of immortality." As king of the gods he represents the power of life that is brought to earth by rainwater and stored by men as semen.

KALI
The Black One

KALI IS THE GODDESS OF DISSOLUTION and destruction who puts an end to all illusion. She is called the Black One, for she is like the darkest night that swallows everything. She is frightening in appearance, with wild eyes, a tongue that hangs out, and dreadful teeth. She is depicted standing on a corpse while wielding a bloody sword and holding the severed head of a demon in her hand.

Her most famous battle was with the demon Raktabija, whom the gods could not kill. Every drop of his blood that touched the ground transformed itself into another demon. Within a few minutes of attacking him with their weapons, the gods would find the entire battlefield covered with millions of demon clones.

In despair, the gods turned to Shiva, but Shiva was lost in meditation. So they approached Parvati, who immediately set out to do battle with the dreaded demon. To protect herself, she took the fearful form of Kali.

As Kali rode onto the battleground on her lion, the evil Raktabija became afraid for the first time in his life. Kali ordered the gods to attack him while she spread her enormous tongue over the battlefield, thus preventing a single drop of blood from falling on the ground. Raktabija was killed. Drunk on his blood, Kali ran across the cosmos killing anyone who dared cross her path.

Kali is usually depicted as an old woman with an insatiable hunger for life. The bowl she holds in her left hand is formed of a human skull and is full to the brim with blood. Her dark color is the color of the earth that creates life through constant destruction.

Kali adorned herself with the heads, limbs, and entrails of her victims. To stop her, Shiva threw himself under her feet. Kali calmed down, embraced him, and shed her ferocious form.

LAKSHMI
Goddess of Fortune

LAKSHMI PERSONIFIES FORTUNE, WEALTH, loveliness, and grace. She is the consort of Vishnu and represents liberation from the cycle of life and death.

Although chosen by Vishnu to be his consort, Lakshmi remained an avid devotee of Shiva. Every day she had a thousand flowers plucked by her handmaidens, and in the evening she offered them at an altar for Shiva. One day, she counted two less than a thousand. It was too late to pick any more, for evening had come and the flowers had all closed their petals for the night.

Thinking it inauspicious to offer less than a thousand, she suddenly remembered that Vishnu had once described her breasts as blooming lotuses. She decided to offer them as the two missing flowers.

She proceeded to cut off the first breast. Before she could cut off the second, Shiva appeared, extremely moved by her devotion, and asked her to stop. He then turned her cut breast into the round bael fruit and sent it to earth with his blessings, to flourish near his temples.

Lakshmi was notorious for consorting freely with various gods and had a reputation for fickleness and inconstancy. In one text it is said that she is so unsteady that even in a picture she moves. Thus she is known as the Restless One.

Lakshmi is often associated with the lotus. Rooted in the mud but blossoming above the water, the lotus represents spiritual perfection. To be seated upon the lotus suggests transcendence. Lakshmi thus represents a state of detachment that transcends the material world.

Lakshmi, like most gods and goddesses, is always aged sixteen, the number of perfection. In humans, it is after the age of sixteen that the first elements of decay begin to appear. When the moon reaches its sixteenth day, it begins to decrease.

PARVATI
Daughter of the Mountain

"PARVAT" MEANS MOUNTAIN. Parvati, daughter of Himavan, god of the Himalayas, is known as Daughter of the Mountain. Her greatest pleasure is to serve Shiva, and she combines the roles of caring wife and affectionate mother.

Shiva is passionate in his love for Parvati. Of the many games they play together, one is a game of dice. Once, Parvati was losing to Shiva, but gradually the tables turned and Shiva lost everything he had staked in the game, including the crescent moon and all his jewels. When Parvati demanded that Shiva give her what she had won, the two fought. Parvati stood her ground and removed everything from Shiva, including his loincloth. This enraged Shiva and he stalked off into the wilderness, leaving Parvati behind.

Tormented by the separation, she soon went in search of Shiva. Taking the form of another woman, she approached the meditating Shiva. He opened his eyes and, feeling attracted to this beautiful woman, jumped up. When he realized that she was none other than Parvati, he laughed and fell into her arms.

The association between Parvati and Shiva is often seen to represent the perennial tension between the ideals of the ascetic and the householder. Parvati's aim is to lure Shiva into the world of marriage, sex, and children, to tempt him away from asceticism, yoga, and otherworldly preoccupations. In this role she is cast as a figure who enhances life in the world, who represents the beauty and attraction of worldly, sexual life, and who cherishes the home and the family.

Parvati sits with Shiva on a throne talking with their son Karttikeya, who was born when a drop of Shiva's semen, which had fallen on the floor, was taken away by a bird and implanted in the combined wombs of seven women.

SARASVATI
Goddess of Wisdom

SARASVATI'S CHARACTER AND ATTRIBUTES are clearly associated with the Sarasvati River. In a symbolic sense she suggests the sacredness of rivers or of water in general. Sarasvati is said to bestow fertility and riches, for her waters enrich the land so that it can produce. Like water, she also represents purity.

Early literature describes Sarasvati as a goddess of speech. The entire process of creation is said to have originated in the vibration of sound. A mantra, which consists of sacred sounds, possesses great power, and the mantra of any particular god is thought to be equivalent to the god himself. To chant a mantra is to make the god present.

As the embodiment of speech, Sarasvati is present wherever speech is present, and when a child is born it is common for the grandmother to use honey to make a five-pointed star, called a *sarasvati*, on the baby's tongue.

Sarasvati's color is white, the color of peace. Her clothes, the lotus she sits upon, and her familiar swan are all white. Her appearance is graceful and serene and shows a total lack of artifice.

When she was first created, Brahma grew angry at her because she kept eluding his advances. We do not know how, but legend has it that he managed to marry her. Lore also has it that his young wife was too aloof and absentminded for his liking. Once, when he had arranged for a major fire sacrifice at which his wife's appearance was required, he repeatedly warned her not to take too long over her toilet, for he was concerned that she would miss the auspicious hour. But Sarasvati, with her characteristic

Sarasvati is a water deity and is symbolic of the pool of knowledge that runs parallel to creation. In the form of a river she runs from the mountains to the sea, moving through and nourishing all the realms of human existence.

disregard for Brahma's desire, prolonged her toilet and was late for the appointment. When she finally arrived, a furious Brahma threw her out, replacing her with Gayatri, the daughter of a sage.

Sarasvati, though married, never enjoyed domestic bliss. According to most myths she had no children, possessed a fiery temper, was easily provoked, and was somewhat quarrelsome. She is described as having a very independent will and never being very obliging to the male gods.

As the disinherited daughter and estranged wife, Sarasvati lived in a state of self-imposed exile, focusing her gaze upon the distance. Her capacity to recall things without anger or resentment is her great gift to writers, musicians, and the creators of various art forms—all of whom fight with tradition.

Sarasvati's ironic eye watches Kali's tussle for power against male demons and Lakshmi's subterfuges in the male world of power. But she remains a witness, a dispassionate historian. She is the one who believes in the ultimate futility both of all warfare and of the trappings of wealth.

SOMA
God of the Moon

"SOMA" IS THE NECTAR OF THE GODS, the elixir of immortality, the cure-all for any injury. It is said to have sprung forth with the churning of the ocean. As a god, Soma represents ecstasy, and his nectar, *amrita*, was the food of the gods.

Soma is also known as the god of the moon and is represented as a copper-colored man carrying a red pennant behind a chariot drawn either by an antelope or by ten white horses. He is the son of the Lord of the Oceans, from which the moon rises. During half the month the gods feed on Soma's

Because the intoxicating juice of the *soma* plant seemed to lend supernatural powers to those who drank it, it was worshipped as a god. Soma symbolizes the replacement of ordinary pleasure with the pleasure of divine bliss.

nectar to retain their immortality. He becomes so exhausted that he wastes away as the moon wanes. Then, fed with water from the ocean, he regains his strength and rises as the moon grows full.

Soma is the all-powerful god who gave Indra the strength to conquer his enemy Vrita, the snake of darkness.

He is said to have forty-three wives—all sisters—of which one named Rohini had been his favorite. Being dissatisfied with the partiality shown to Rohini, the rest of the sisters returned to their home. When Soma asked them to come back, their father consented, provided Soma would treat them all alike. Soma promised to do this, but failing to keep his promise, he was smitten with consumption for breaking his word.

At one time, feeling very arrogant and licentious, Soma carried off Tara, the wife of the teacher Vrihaspati. In vain Vrihaspati tried to recover his bride and appealed to Brahma, who commanded Soma to return the woman. Soma wouldn't listen. A great battle erupted, the gods fighting together on one side to recover Tara, with Soma and the demons on the other side.

The gods won the battle, but upon her return to Vrihaspati, he found that she was pregnant. He refused to receive her until the child was born. She immediately bore a beautiful son, whom both Vrihaspati and Soma claimed as their own. Tara was too ashamed to speak.

The child was indignant at this and said to her, "Unless you tell me who my father is, I will sentence you to a fate that will deter every female from ever hesitating to speak the truth." At this Brahma interfered, pacifying the child and saying to Tara, "Tell me, is this the child of Vrihaspati or Soma?"

"Of Soma," she answered, blushing. As soon as she had spoken Soma, puffed up with pride and joy, embraced his son.

VISHVAKARMAN
Architect of the Universe

VISHVAKARMAN IS THE SON OF BRAHMA and the personification of the creative power that keeps heaven and earth together. It was Vishvakarman who discovered the sciences of both architecture and mechanics. He is the official architect of all of the gods' palaces and the designer of their flying chariots and weapons.

According to legend, his daughter Sanjana was married to Surya, the sun. Since she was not able to endure his heat and his light, Vishvakarman placed Surya upon his lathe and cut away an eighth part of his brightness. The fragments that fell on the earth were used by Vishvakarman to form the various weapons of the gods.

In his process of creation, Vishvakarman once performed a special sacrifice, in which he offered up all the creatures and ultimately himself, too. This represents the ultimate sacrifice of the self that is integral to the creation of the greater universe in the heart of the devoted one.

Epilogue

Those who worship the gods become gods; those who worship ancestors become ancestors; those who worship the elements master the elements; and those who worship me gain me.
　　　—Bhagavad Gita 9.25

WE BECOME WHAT WE WORSHIP. To a Hindu, worship is an attitude of devotion. It is an inner space, not an act. When God becomes an inner reality, we are free.

The gods of Hinduism are part of the inner life of those who hold them sacred. They are recognized in their fullness when all separations between the seeker and the sought, between devotee and God, have disappeared. The reality of this recognition is known to many under many different names. It is a state of absolute freedom and happiness.

One of the most profound aspects of the stories of the Hindu gods is the lightheartedness with which they can be told. Life is a *leela*, a divine

Krishna embodies love—its pleasure and its compassion as well as love's ability to overcome all odds. Stories of Krishna's amorous escapades, and the emotions that are played out within them, have become the inspiration behind much of India's great poetry and art. He represents the perfect union not only of the love between a man and a woman but between the individual and our earth, our existence.

dance. It goes around, as all of nature goes around, in a spiral of joy. It is the great creation that we participate in by creating its story.

Everything is just imaginary, say some. Life is nothing but the dreaming of gods. When the dreamer goes to sleep the world is his.

Joyful and penetrating, whimsical and sometimes disturbing, the stories of the Hindu gods are part of the fabric of life. Their stories take their meaning from our everyday situations. Their complex personalities are drawn from the subtleties of the human heart, which longs to reunite with God. Informing, revealing, they breathe meaning into small things, drawing humans ever closer to their world and to nirvana, the state of absolute freedom.

CREDITS

Alvin O. Bellak Collection, Philadelphia: pp. 8, 17, 21, 26, 36, 40, 51, 56, 59, 60, 71, 80, 84

British Museum, London: pp. 2, 34, 48, 83

Institute of Oriental Studies, St. Petersburg: pp. 18, 25, 29, 43, 44, 66, 75, 76, 87

Los Angeles County Museum of Art, Los Angeles: pp. 11, 14, 22, 33, 52, 55, 63, 68, 79, 88, 92, 95

Philadelphia Musuem of Art, Philadelphia: p. 72

Special thanks to Professor Robert DeCaroli for his care and thoughtfulness, and to all those who, in my travels to India, have so enriched my life.